TRIBES of NATIVE AMERICA

Navajo

edited by Marla Felkins Ryan
and Linda Schmittroth

BLACKBIRCH®
PRESS

THOMSON
———✦———
GALE

San Diego • Detroit • New York • San Francisco • Cleveland
New Haven, Conn. • Waterville, Maine • London • Munich

THOMSON
━━━━★━━━━ ™
GALE

© 2002 by Blackbirch Press™. Blackbirch Press™ is an imprint of The Gale Group, Inc., a division of Thomson Learning, Inc.

Blackbirch Press™ and Thomson Learning™ are trademarks used herein under license.

For more information, contact
The Gale Group, Inc.
27500 Drake Rd.
Farmington Hills, MI 48331-3535
Or you can visit our Internet site at http://www.gale.com

Photo credits: Cover Courtesy of Northwestern University Library; cover © National Archives; cover © Photospin; cover © Perry Jasper Photography; cover © Picturequest; cover © Seattle Post-Intelligencer Collection, Museum of History & Industry; cover © Blackbirch Press Archives; cover © Library of Congress; cover © PhotoDisc; pages 5, 6, 7, 8, 13, 14, 16, 17, 18, 19, 21, 23, 24, 25, 26, 30 © CORBIS; pages 9, 10 © Hulton Archive; pages 15, 19, 20, 21, 22 © Western History/Genealogy Department, Denver Public Library; pages 18, 23, 27, 29 © AP/Wide World

LIBRARY OF CONGRESS CATALOGING-IN-PUBLICATION DATA

Navajo / Marla Felkins Ryan, book editor; Linda Schmittroth, book editor.
    v. cm. — (Tribes of Native America)
Includes bibliographical references and index.
Contents: Name — Origins and group affiliations — The Navajo code talkers — Language — Economy — Daily life — Education — Customs — Current tribal issues.
    ISBN 1-56711-624-8 (alk. paper)
    1. Navajo Indians—Juvenile literature. [1. Navajo Indians. 2. Indians of North America—Southwest, New.] I. Ryan, Marla Felkins. II. Schmittroth, Linda. III. Series.
    E99.N3 N279 2003
    979.1004'972—dc21   2002008670

Table of Contents

NAVAJO

Name

The name Navajo (pronounced *NAH-vah-ho*) comes from a Tewa Indian word that means "cultivated fields." The Navajo call themselves Diné ("the People").

Navajo Nation Today

Federal reservation: 26,000 square miles of former homelands in northeastern Arizona, northwestern New Mexico, and southeastern Utah

Darker shaded area: Navajo Nation

Lighter shaded area: Hopi Nation, surrounded by Navajo Nation

Where are the traditional Navajo lands?

The Navajo live on a reservation called the Navajo Nation. It is the largest reservation in the United States. It includes more than 26,000 square miles of old Navajo lands in northeastern Arizona, northwestern New Mexico, and southeastern Utah.

What has happened to the population?

In 1868, there were about 10,000 Navajo. In a 1990 population count by the U.S. Bureau of the Census, 225,298 people said they were Navajo.

Navajo Population From 1868 to Today

POPULATION

300,000

200,000

100,000

0

1868   1990

YEAR

Navajo children at Canyon de Chelly, ancestral lands in Arizona

Origins and group ties

Stories of Navajo history tell of the First World (or Black World). This was a frigid, flatland area, perhaps in Alaska. The Second World (or Blue-Green World) had landmarks and animal life like those found in western and central Canada. The Third World (or Yellow World) had mountains and plains like those on the eastern slope of the Rocky Mountains and the Southwest. The Fourth World (or Glittering World) was like what is now northwestern New Mexico.

Navajo traditions recount the steady movement of the Navajo people to the Southwest.

The Navajo people have kept more of their culture than most other tribes. Today, nine out of ten Navajo continue to live on reservation lands.

The Navajo people have maintained much of their native culture.

HISTORY

Outside influences

Spaniards came to Navajo land in the 17th century. The Navajo had been hunters and gatherers. From around 1650 to 1775, however, they learned from the Spanish and the Pueblo Indians how to farm corn, herd sheep, weave wool, and work silver. The Spanish taught them how to grow new fruits and vegetables, such as peaches, wheat, and potatoes. Spaniards also introduced the Navajo to cattle, sheep, and horses.

Beginning in the late 1600s, the Navajo moved westward into what are now New Mexico and Arizona. The tribe joined with the Pueblo and Apache to fight the Spanish. Around 1750, the Navajo set up a fortified town in Canyon de Chelly.

This Navajo cave painting in Canyon de Chelly, Arizona, shows Spanish conquerors on horseback.

Americans fought against Santa Anna's soldiers in the Mexican-American War from 1846 to 1848.

The U.S. government and the Navajo

In the early 1800s, Spanish colonists in the Southwest rebelled against Spain. They then founded the nation of Mexico. Although they claimed to own the northern territory where the Navajo lived, most Mexicans lived farther south. The United States took over most of the Southwest in 1848, after it won the Mexican-American War (1846–1848). At first, the Americans tried to sign peace treaties with the Navajo. The Americans wrongly thought, however, that the leaders of the Navajo bands who signed treaties could act for all Navajo. In fact, each leader could speak only for his own band.

When bands that had not signed treaties made raids, Americans thought their agreements had been violated. In 1864, the U.S. government

1917–1918
WWI fought in Europe

1923
The Navajo unite under a tribal council

1929
Stock market crash begins the Great Depression

1941
Bombing at Pearl Harbor forces United States into WWII

1941-1945
Navajo Code Talkers send and receive secret messages in their native language, a major part of the U.S. war effort in World War II

1945
WWII ends

1950s
Reservations no longer controlled by federal government

1974
Congress passes the Navajo-Hopi Land Settlement Act. It creates a Joint Use Area and requires individual tribe members to move to their own tribal lands

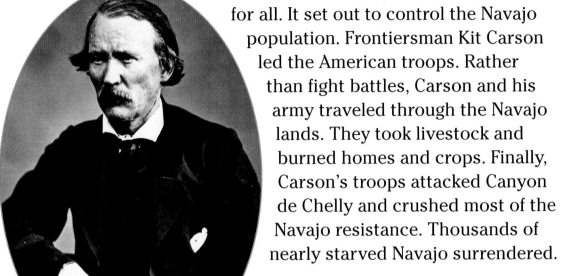

decided to settle the problem once and for all. It set out to control the Navajo population. Frontiersman Kit Carson led the American troops. Rather than fight battles, Carson and his army traveled through the Navajo lands. They took livestock and burned homes and crops. Finally, Carson's troops attacked Canyon de Chelly and crushed most of the Navajo resistance. Thousands of nearly starved Navajo surrendered.

American frontiersman Kit Carson helped remove the Navajo from their homes and native lands.

The Long Walk

In 1864, more than 8,000 Navajo were resettled at a place called Bosque (pronounced BOSK) Redondo. It was located near Fort Sumner in east-central New Mexico. They made the 300-mile trip on foot in an event known as the Long Walk. Those who could not keep up were either sent into slavery or shot by guards. Those who complained of illness were also shot. This included women who were about to give birth. More than 2,000 Navajo died.

Once they arrived at the 40-square-acre reservation, the Navajo found that the land was not good for growing food. The water was bad. There was little firewood. There were also plagues of insects. Yet on this land, the Navajo were expected to become farmers. At the same time, the Navajo faced raids by their Indian enemies. More than 2,000 Navajo died from starvation and disease. Only about half of the Navajo lived through their time at Bosque Redondo.

The U.S. government at first did little to help the sick and dying Navajo. Then, a newspaper wrote about the conditions on the reservation. In time, the government admitted that the resettlement had been a mistake. In 1868, Congress set up a reservation on original Navajo lands and invited the Navajo to return from Bosque Redondo. The Navajo, however, were only allowed to come to an area called Treaty Reservation. It was made up of just 10 percent of their former lands. The area was surrounded by non-Indians who had moved in while the Navajo were gone.

The four reservations

The 3.5-million-acre Navajo Nation reservation expanded over time with land grants. It now includes more than 17 million acres.

After they left Bosque Redondo, three bands of Navajo settled apart from the main tribe. They set up three small reservations in western New Mexico. Today, more than 5,000 Navajo live on the Ramah, the Cañoncito, and the Alamo reservations.

The twentieth century

Many Navajo volunteered to fight in World War I (1914–1918). In 1924, all Indians were made U.S. citizens, in large part because of the service of Indian soldiers in World War I.

The Navajo also made a major contribution in World War II (1939–1945). Men called Code Talkers used the Navajo language to send secret messages for the U.S. military.

Land dispute with the Hopi

Since their reservations were founded, the Navajo and Hopi had a land dispute. The Navajo Nation used only 10 percent of the tribe's original land. The Hopi reservation was created next to the Navajo Nation in 1882. In 1934, Congress expanded the Navajo reservation. It then completely surrounded the Hopi reservation. Each tribe thought land given to the other should be its own.

In 1962, a federal court ruling made an area around Hopi land a Joint Use Area (JUA) for both tribes. When oil and coal were found in the JUA, the tribes were even more eager for a clear decision on ownership. The Navajo-Hopi Settlement Act of 1974 allowed for the division of the JUA between the two tribes. It also required people who lived on the other tribe's land to move. This applied to nearly 10,000

THE NAVAJO CODE TALKERS

After the United States entered World War II (1939–1945), it learned that its Japanese enemies could decode secret U.S. messages. In early 1942, a white man who had lived at the Navajo Nation suggested that the Navajo language be used for codes. It would be very hard to break. Other than the 50,000 Navajo, not more than 30 people in the world knew the language. None of those people was Japanese.

Young Navajo men became Code Talkers. Because the Navajo language had no words for military terms, Code Talker Carl Gorman and others worked out a two-step code. In it, English military words were represented by different Navajo words. For example, kinds of planes were called by Navajo words for kinds of birds. The Japanese eventually figured out that the code was Navajo. They tried to force a captured soldier who spoke the language to translate. He could not do so, however. Though he knew that a term such as *chay-da-gahi* meant "turtle," he did not know that *turtle* meant "tank" to the Code Talkers.

Navajo soldiers sent and received messages in their native language during WWII.

Navajo. Many who had to move could not find work. In time, one-third of them lost their new homes.

The dispute neared an end in 1997. The Navajo who still lived on Hopi land could stay in their homes if they signed a 75-year lease and agreed to accept Hopi rules. It was a difficult choice. The Navajo would have to ask for Hopi permission to conduct many of their ceremonies. They would also not be allowed to bury their dead on the leased land. Despite these limitations, most Navajo signed the lease in March 1997.

This sacred painting made from colored sand shows a Navajo god.

Religion

The Navajo strive for harmony with nature and other people. They believe that everything, no matter how tiny, has an important place in the universe.

Among the Navajo gods are many Holy People. These include Changing Woman (who created the People), Spider Woman (who taught the People to weave), Talking God (who taught the People to build houses), and Coyote (a prankster who taught many lessons). Ceremonies called Blessing Ways give thanks for a long and happy life or celebrate a new house or marriage.

Mountain Earth bundles are the most important ceremonial objects. They are made of tanned buckskin taken from a deer killed in a special ritual. The bundle holds small pouches of soil and other items. These are brought from the top of the four sacred mountains that surround Navajo lands.

Navajo Christians

Over the years, various Christian groups tried to convert the Navajo. In the late 1860s and 1870s, Presbyterian and Mormon missionaries had a presence on the reservation. In the 1890s, Catholic priests began a mission. They later opened a school that studied Navajo culture. Protestant faiths also opened churches and schools, and many Navajo became Christians.

Navajo children pose in front of a Methodist mission in Farmington, New Mexico.

A medicine man prepares for a ceremony.

Present-day Navajo often mix Christianity with traditional beliefs. About 25,000 Navajo belong to the Native American Church. Their belief system focuses on visions that come through dreams, prayers, rituals, and the peyote (pronounced pay-O-tee) plant. Peyote comes from cactus. When it is eaten, it causes a trance-like state in which a person might see visions.

Government

Until modern times, the tribe had no overall structure. It was made up of small, independent bands led by chiefs or headmen. The discovery of coal and oil at the Navajo Nation around 1920 made it necessary for the tribe to reorganize. The Navajo Business Council was founded in 1922 by the U.S. government. Its job was to grant oil and mineral leases.

In 1938, the Navajo rejected the Indian Reorganization Act (IRA). This law would have given them a federally structured tribal government and

constitution. Instead, they wrote their own constitution. It aimed to give them independence from the federal Bureau of Indian Affairs (BIA). The U.S. government rejected this plan. Instead, it formed a new Navajo Business Council. The council was made up of 74 elected Navajo and became known as the Rule of 1938. It formed the basis for today's Navajo Tribal Council.

Navajo council members address political concerns at the Navajo tribal government center in Window Rock, Arizona.

Farms and ranches

Traditionally, the Navajo were farmers who did not water their fields. Over time, farming methods have changed. In the 1960s, Congress approved the Navajo Irrigation Implementation Project (NIIP). It used canals, pipelines, pumping stations, and sprinklers to water crops.

Ranching, too, has changed. Since the 17th century, sheep herding was a vital part of Navajo life. In the late 1930s, an extreme drought made the central and southern United States very dry. The area came to be called the Dust Bowl. The U.S. government thought that the Navajo's sheep would strip plant cover off topsoil as they grazed. The topsoil would then dry out and blow away. To

The Navajo Agriculture Products Industry has brought green crops to the otherwise dry Navajo reservation.

A shepherd tends a flock of sheep. Sheep herding remains an important part of the Navajo tradition.

prevent this, the Agricultural Department killed tens of thousands of sheep. During the 20th century, cattle ranches largely replaced the business of sheep herding on the reservation.

Other ways to earn money

Today, the Navajo Nation leases its land for gas and oil drilling. It also makes money through coal mining, forestry, and industrial parks. There are more than 250

Petroleum workers adjust an oil drill on Navajo land.

A Navajo woman weaves on a blanket loom.

other trade operations that rely on the use of reservation land. They include shopping centers and banks.

Navajo weavers command high prices for their traditional handmade woolen rugs, belts, and blankets. Other native craftspeople make silver bracelets, rings, earrings, necklaces, and belts decorated with turquoise stones.

A craftsman makes silver jewelry.

DAILY LIFE

This mother and her twins are part of a Navajo clan.

Families

Navajo society is based on clans (groups of people who have a common ancestor). The original clans were Towering House, Bitterwater, Big Water, and One-who-walks-around. Other clans arose when new groups became part of the Navajo tribe.

Buildings

Traditional Navajo houses are called hogans. Older hogans were cone-shaped. In the mid-1800s, log cabins with beehive-shaped log roofs became more popular. The roof and walls were often covered with packed earth. A smoke hole was left at the center of the roof. When wood was scarce, hogans were built of stones held together with mud mortar.

In recent years, modern cinderblock houses have become more common. Other structures at Navajo homes include corrals made of brush and open-walled work spaces with flat roofs.

Newly built hogans are sprinkled with corn pollen or meal. Prayers are then said to bring the home happiness. Hogan doors must face eastward, toward the rising sun.

The roof and walls of this hogan are covered with packed earth.

Hogan doors must face eastward.

A Navajo woman at the turn of the 20th century wears richly colored clothes and turquoise jewelry.

Clothing

Early Navajo men wore breechcloths (flaps of material that cover the front and back and hang from the waist). Navajo also wore leggings, skirts, and blankets woven from the yucca plant or cedar bark, or made of fur. Animal skins were used to make moccasins with braided yucca soles. By the early 17th century, men wore tanned buckskin. Women wore dresses made of fabrics such as wool. By the time of the Long Walk, clothing had become quite colorful.

Men wore knee-length buckskin pants with brass and silver buttons along the outer seams. Woolen leggings dyed blue and decorated with bright red garters completed the outfit. Women wore ankle-length dresses. They also wore leggings made from strips of dyed buckskin wrapped around the legs and decorated with silver buttons.

During the late 19th and early 20th centuries, women wore long, full skirts of cotton with bright blouses. Men wore jeans, colorful shirts, and boots. Their belts were decorated with silver disks, and their headbands were made of rolled kerchiefs. Both men and women traditionally wore their hair long. Their hair was wound into an hourglass shape at the base of the neck.

Food

When they first moved to the Southwest, the Navajo hunted and gathered wild plants for food. They soon learned how to grow crops such as corn, beans, and squash. The Spanish taught them to grow wheat and oats, and to herd sheep and goats. By the time they went to Bosque Redondo, the Navajo often ate sheep meat, corn, frybread (disks of bread fried in hot fat), and coffee with sugar and goat's milk. They also ate mush made from cornmeal or wild seed mixed with water or goat's milk.

Navajo frybread sizzles in an iron frying pan.

Education

Navajo children watched their parents and other adults to learn life skills. In the 19th century, the Navajo opposed efforts to start white-style schools for their children. They saw the

A teenager studies Navajo with the help of a teacher in New Mexico.

schools as a threat to their way of life. Some children were sent away to boarding schools. There, they were taught to speak and dress like whites.

Today, the Navajo Nation has state schools that serve kindergarten through twelfth grade, as well as several Bureau of Indian Affairs boarding schools.

Healing practices

For the Navajo, sickness is a sign of disharmony. Illnesses can be caused by breaking a social rule, by contact with a ghost, or by a witch's spell.

When a person gets sick, he or she goes to a person called a stargazer or hand trembler. This person determines the cause of the illness. The stargazer then recommends a medicine person known

A medicine man uses a sandpainting to try to heal a patient's illness.

as a Hataali (singer). The Hataali holds a ceremony in which the patient and his or her relatives take part. It may last as many as nine nights and include more than 500 songs. Sometimes there are also dancers who wear masks that stand for certain spirits. The healer may use objects with special powers and medicines made from plants. Most curing rituals are followed by the singing of the "Blessing Way." This prayer has been called the backbone of the Navajo healing system. As many parts of Navajo culture have broken down, some modern institutions have begun to teach native healing arts.

Navajo are skillful at making beautiful coiled baskets. Some of them are woven so tightly that they can hold water.

Today, Indian Health Service hospitals on the reservation have special rooms where medicine men conduct traditional curing ceremonies. This new spirit of cooperation between modern and traditional medical people brings more Navajo in for treatment.

Craftwork

Navajo women have long been known for their excellent pottery. Their pottery included ladles, jars with pointed bottoms, and decorated bowls. They also made coiled baskets, food containers, and water bottles. In addition, they wove rugs and blankets with intricate designs, colored with natural dyes.

CUSTOMS

Taboos

Children are instructed in ritual dances that are an important part of Navajo celebrations.

The Navajo believe that the order of the world must be maintained to ward off illness or other bad luck. This is done, in part, through a large assortment of taboos (forbidden things or acts). There are thousands of taboos. Among them are rules that say lightning-struck trees must not be touched, and that people should never comb their hair at night.

Puberty

Girls go through kinaald. This is a two-day ritual designed to teach them the skills they will need as adults. In it, a girl must perform several exhausting runs to prove her physical condition and endurance. She must then grind by hand some of the cornmeal and wheat she will use to make a traditional cake. As she works, a medicine man chants prayers. Near the end of the ceremony, a female relative massages the girl's body. Then the girl prays over a group of young children. After the ritual, the girl is seen as an adult who is ready for marriage.

Ceremonies and Festivals

The War Dance is officially called "The Enemyway." It may be the most common Navajo ceremony. It is a three-day event held in summer that is a way for a person to get rid of the effects of some enemy. For example, it may be held for people who feel weak, faint from the sight of blood, or who have nightmares. The ceremony uses a carved piece of juniper about 18 inches long, called a Rattle Stick. Burnt herbs and melted wax are placed on the stick and on the face of the sufferer. During the complicated ceremony, the enemy's ghost is killed and its ashes are scattered. Then there is a big feast and dance.

Rodeo is a popular element of Navajo festivals.

A number of fairs, festivals, and rodeos are also held. They feature sandpainting, songs, and dances. They also use cornmeal, corn pollen, feathered prayer sticks, and bundles of sacred items.

Courtship and marriage

Relatives usually arrange marriages. Often an expensive gift (such as sheep or horses) is given to the girl's family by the boy's family. When a couple marries, the grandmother of the bride gives the new couple a basket of cornmeal. The bride and groom exchange a pinch of the cornmeal to win the blessing of the spirit world.

Newly married couples usually live near the wife's mother's home. This lets the wife and children have close contact with the maternal grandmother. A large space is left between the houses, however. This is because a man is not allowed to look at or speak to his mother-in-law.

Funerals

In past times, the Navajo had many funeral rituals. Right after the death of a family member, close relatives began to mourn. They wept, cut their hair, and put on old clothing. Elderly relatives dressed the deceased in fine clothes. Burial took place in the daytime, as soon as possible. The corpse was placed with many personal possessions on a horse, and taken far away. The grave was a crevice in the rocks that could be covered with brush. The horse was killed at the gravesite, so the dead person could use it in the afterworld.

All the mourners burned sage, or some other strong-smelling plant. They then bathed in the smoke. The rest of the deceased's possessions were broken or burned. Nothing was kept that would remind the living of the dead person. The name of the deceased was never mentioned again.

Current tribal issues

One recent issue has dealt with a 7,000-square-mile area known as the Checkerboard. When railroads were built in the late 1800s, land in this region was granted to railroad companies. Federal programs in the early 20th century further broke up the area. Today, nearly 30,000 Navajo live in the Checkerboard. The tribe hopes to trade or buy land so that larger parcels can be put together.

Peterson Zah, followed by his wife, attends his inauguration as tribal chairman in 1983. The ceremony was conducted in Navajo and English.

Notable people

Peterson Zah (1937–) has served as chief executive officer of the Navajo Nation government and chief fundraiser for the Navajo Education and Scholarship Foundation. In 1988, he founded a private firm that provided educational services to school districts. He also raised money to build new reservation schools.

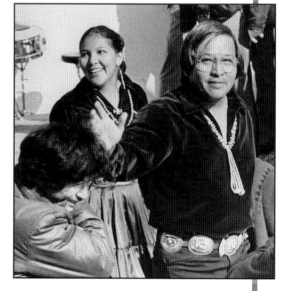

Annie Dodge Wauneka (1910–1997) was the first woman elected to the Navajo Tribal Council. In 1964, she became the first Native American to receive the Presidential Medal of Freedom.

Manuelito (1818–1894) was a powerful warrior in raids against the Mexicans, Hopi, and Zuñi. He later traveled to Washington, D.C., to ask for the return of Navajo lands. He served as principal Navajo chief and chief of tribal police.

Henry Chee Dodge (c. 1857–1947) helped form a modern identity for the Navajo Nation. Under his leadership, the tribe began to work with the federal government to make and carry out policies for mineral development, land rights issues, and other programs.

Other notable Navajo include: war chief Barboncito (c. 1820–1871); nuclear physicist and professor Fred Begay (1932–); painter Harrison Begay (1917–); artist and Code Talker Carl Nelson

Manuelito was a powerful war chief. He tried to get the government to return Navajo lands to his tribe.

Gorman (1907–1998); artist R. C. Gorman (1931–); educator and tribal councilman Ned Hatathli (1923–1972); tribal chairperson Peter MacDonald (1928-); tribal leader Raymond Nakai (1918–); and award-winning poet Luci Tapahonso (1953–).

For More Information

Dutton, Bertha P. *Indians of the American Southwest.* Englewood Cliffs, NJ: Prentice-Hall, 1975.

Gilpin, Laura. *The Enduring Navajo.* Austin, TX: University of Texas Press, 1968.

Iverson, Peter. *The Navajos.* New York: Chelsea House Publishers, 1990.

Osinski, Alice. *The Navajo.* Chicago, IL: Childrens Press, 1987.

Trimble, Stephen. *The People: Indians of the American Southwest.* Santa Fe, NM: School of American Research Press, 1993.

Official website for the Navajo Nation www.navajo.org

Glossary

Reservation land set aside and given to Native Americans

Ritual something that is custom or done in a certain way

Sacred highly valued and important

Shaman a priest or priestess who uses magic for the purpose of curing the sick, learning the unknown, and controlling events

Tradition a custom or an established pattern of behavior

Treaty agreement

Tribe a group of people who live together in a community

Index